For Virginia
with best

John

AUGUST 2013

# THE BRUNELS
*Engineers Extraordinaire*

Great Western Railway – interior of the Box Tunnel

# THE BRUNELS

*Engineers Extraordinaire*

A celebration in verse

John Byrne

STANSFIELD

THE BRUNELS
*Engineers Extraordinaire*

First published in 2013 by
Stansfield
71 Pevensey Road
London SW17 OHT

stansfield303@gmail.com

© John Byrne 2013
Designed by Pete MacKenzie

British Library Cataloguing in Publication Data
A catalogue entry of this book is available from the British Library

ISBN 978-0-9574493-0-5

Printed in Great Britain by
Short Run Press Limited
Exeter EX2 7LW

All rights reserved. No part of this publication may be reproduced, stored in a retrieval system, or transmitted in any form or by any means, electronic, mechanical, photocopying, recording or otherwise, without the prior permission of the copyright holder.

*To Christine,*

*thank you for travelling this five year journey with me*

11 April 1845

*It occurs to me to mention a point which may influence the Board in requesting my attendance, the subject of my professional charges. I think it better if there can be no possibility of disappointment. I have long since given up any mode of travelling, when off the railway, except in my own carriage. When I tell you that I shall probably come up from Bristol to London on Sunday night, that I go to Exeter on Monday night, return on Tuesday night to go to Ely (if I go) on Wednesday and return to London on Thursday night, you will not be surprised that, to enable me to lead such a life I am obliged to adopt every means for diminishing fatigue. I mention this that no misunderstanding may arise as I hate extravagance as much as those who have to pay for it. If I come to Ely I would want to get away to Wisbech and then to Peterborough by daylight and make full use of the day.*

I. K. Brunel

# CONTENTS

| | |
|---|---|
| Introduction | 1 |
| Nonchalant Navigation | 7 |
| Emigré | 8 |
| Dig First, Think Later! | 9 |
| Seizing Life | 11 |
| Sharp Practice | 12 |
| Way Beneath | 13 |
| Unrealised | 14 |
| Ultimate Bore | 15 |
| Short Cut | 16 |
| Teredo Navalis | 17 |
| The Rainhill Rattler | 18 |
| Health and Safety | 19 |
| 'Cannon Can be Nothing to it' | 20 |
| Trial and Tribulation | 21 |
| Canterbury and Whitstable (The Oyster Line 1830) | 23 |
| Young Lion | 24 |
| Clifton Caper | 25 |
| The Highwayman | 27 |
| 'Let Me Try' | 29 |
| Avon Audacity | 30 |
| Telford Tenacity | 31 |
| Suspicious Survey | 32 |
| Iron Dream (1833) | 33 |
| Cock-a-Hoop | 34 |
| Cut and Thrust | 35 |
| Cruel Progress | 36 |

| | |
|---|---|
| Sign of the Times | 37 |
| Industrial Revelation (Stations West) | 38 |
| Cat of Nine Lives | 41 |
| Doctor Dogma | 42 |
| Shipping Lines | 43 |
| Smoke for Sail | 44 |
| Significant Shift in Somerset | 45 |
| Sandcastle Science | 46 |
| Head Start | 47 |
| Maidenhead | 48 |
| 1 in 233 | 49 |
| First Great Western | 50 |
| Pushing Boundaries | 51 |
| It's Not Quite as Broad as it is Narrow | 52 |
| Legendary Letters | 53 |
| When Great Minds Differ | 54 |
| Moles | 55 |
| Silly Money | 56 |
| The Box Brigade | 57 |
| Stress Strain and Temper | 58 |
| Paddington Bare | 59 |
| We of Little Faith | 60 |
| Paternal Perception | 63 |
| 'If I Ever Go Mad' | 64 |
| Amused | 65 |
| 'Upwards of 100 men' | 66 |
| Time Motion Tabled | 67 |
| Graphic Guide | 68 |
| Modification Ramification | 69 |
| In the Vale of the White Horse | 70 |
| Glorious Great Britain | 71 |
| The Engineer | 72 |

| | |
|---|---|
| Nautical Nadir | 73 |
| Under Pressure | 74 |
| Refreshment? | 76 |
| The Ghost of Dundrum Bay | 77 |
| Credible Concept (Devil's Bridge, Uphill) | 78 |
| Gremlins at Newton Abbot | 79 |
| Isambard's Important Industrious Innovative Ivybridge Improvisation Idea Inevitably Implemented Immediately | 80 |
| Railway Racket | 81 |
| Suspension of Belief | 83 |
| The Chepstow Challenge | 84 |
| Travel Fever (1850) | 85 |
| Leviathan | 86 |
| A Meeting of the Board at the Eastern Steam Navigation Company | 88 |
| The Crystal Palace | 89 |
| A Shipwright's Challenge (The Testing of John Scott Russell) | 90 |
| In Order to Aid the Good Works of the Lady With the Lamp | 91 |
| One London Winter | 92 |
| Undignified Demise | 93 |
| Industrial Revelation (King of Iron) | 94 |
| Cathedral | 97 |
| Controlled Launch Paradox | 98 |
| Ship of Dreams | 99 |
| Turner Technique | 101 |
| The Effort of Equals | 102 |
| Georgian Wind Victorian Reign | 103 |
| Watershed | 105 |
| Hamoaze Hurdle | 106 |
| Confounded Conclusion | 107 |

| | |
|---|---|
| A Directive From the Office of | |
|    I K Brunel Esq. Duke Street London | 108 |
| Sabbatical | 109 |
| Sundown | 111 |
| Inevitability | 112 |
| End to End | 113 |
| Passing Era | 114 |
| Earthly Estate | 115 |
| Boycott | 116 |
| American Aberration | 117 |
| Lively Legacy | 118 |
| Dickensian Pied Piper | 119 |
| Falkland Faux Pas | 121 |
| Narrow Minds | 122 |
| Exhibitionism | 123 |
| Dr Beeching Goes off the Rails | 124 |
| Simple Sentiment | 125 |
| Regardless | 126 |
| Monumental | 127 |
| Second Great Western | 128 |
| Sweet September (2010) | 129 |
| | |
| Explanatory Notes: *Historical information supporting* | |
| *many of the poems can be found here.* | 133 |
| | |
| Acknowledgements | 148 |

# INTRODUCTION

When Marc Brunel arrived in England by way of America in 1799, just days before his 30th birthday, he set about establishing himself as an inventor, engineer and businessman. Within a month he had filed the first of seventeen patents. By introduction to key figures in the Navy, he was soon able to file a second patent for a machine to mass produce ships' pulley blocks of which 100,000 were required annually.

At the end of 1802 Brunel moved his young family from London to Portsmouth to oversee installation of the mass production line set up at the Royal Dockyard that would save the Navy thousands of pounds every year. He went on to patent machines capable of turning out a wide range of industrial goods from tin foil to boots for the Army. Interestingly his son Isambard never patented a single idea, believing such action would stunt progress.

The pace of the Industrial Revolution – with its mid-eighteenth century origins at many sites in Wales, at Coalbrookdale in Shropshire and with Messrs. Watt and Boulton at Soho on the outskirts of Birmingham – was, at the turn of the nineteenth century, beginning to quicken. When pioneering Cornishman Richard Trevithick mounted a steam powered device on wheels in 1804, he created a forerunner of the railway engine. George Stephenson built the Stockton & Darlington railway, then the Liverpool & Manchester and designed his famous *Rocket* steam engine, with which he won the Rainhill Trials in 1829. Stephenson merely measured the tracks within local coal mines and built his railways to match their four feet eight and a half inch gauge.

In 1824 Marc Brunel was awarded the contract to build the Thames Tunnel at Rotherhithe. At his father's behest, the work would involve his young son Isambard Kingdom as Resident Engineer. Marc adapted his earlier tunnelling shield in order to make such a daunting task possible. When this project ran into irrecoverable difficulties due to constant flooding four years later, all activity ceased and the bore was sealed, before recommencement many years later, leading finally to a successful completion in 1842.

Isambard Kingdom Brunel successfully applied for the post of Engineer to the Great Western Railway, at the age of 26, and in 1833 set about designing and overseeing the building of their proposed line between London and Bristol to his own specification of seven feet and a quarter inch gauge track. He had questioned the logic of 'standard' gauge and rejected its use as a matter of course, believing correctly that as trains inevitably became faster the wider spread rails would give a smoother and more stable ride. It is interesting to note that just as George Stephenson worked to an already existing measurement, so too Brunel. On a previous visit to Chatham Dockyard where his father had once worked, he observed an internal railway track and made a mental note of its dimension, seven feet across.

The GWR opened in stages and was completed in 1841 at a cost of £6.4 million, almost twice that estimated, due in part to the high standard and extravagance of its architecture and to the many unforeseen engineering problems encountered as work progressed. The troublesome Box Tunnel between Chippenham and Bath, for example, took five years to complete and cost the lives of 'upwards of one hundred men'. Today this splendid railway and the vast majority of its infrastructure is still in place, carrying much heavier and faster trains than was ever envisaged at the time of its conception almost 180 years ago.

The introduction of a canal network at the beginning of the Industrial Revolution owes much to Scottish stonemason and civil engineer Thomas Telford (1757–1834), last of the great canal engineers of the age, who was responsible for over thirty three major canal projects with their many hundreds of beautifully designed bridges and aqueducts.

A natural progression from this early work was his branching into the building of roads towards the end of his career, just before the onset of the railway age in the early 19th century. He once famously forecast that the only function railways would perform would be to bring goods to his canals. The thought of 45 mph trains discharging freight onto 4 mph barges to complete a journey now seems quaint and amusing.

The work of Trevithick, George Stephenson and son Robert, John Braithwaite and the like, in advancing steam locomotive technology, laid the foundations of the great railway age. From the opening of the Stockton & Darlington in 1824 to the proliferation in the 1830s: Liverpool & Manchester, Canterbury & Whitstable, London & Birmingham (the first railway line in the world to serve a capital city), London & Greenwich, London Nine Elms & Southampton, Eastern Counties Railway and of course Brunel's Great Western Railway...

Great Western Railway – view near Chippenham

Great Western Railway – entrance to the tunnel at Box

## Nonchalant Navigation

Swift or swallow matters not
Hand dug canal in summer bathes
Heavy horse on coal barge tether
Man and beast great minds together
Through floral meadow cutting swathes

'cross valley floor on high arched brick
Down gradient levelled multi-lock
Modernistic transportation
Great pride of a generation
Leisurely tick, the Georgian clock

Cool the breeze through stooping willow
Slight the dew September morn
Midland town built red brick plain
The vital hub within a chain
Receiving, sending, waterborne

Expansion east, progression west
An air of safe stability
Confident complacent days
Wealthy toll rich waterways
Sheer invincibility?

**Emigré**

Echappant aux feux de l'enfer de Rouen
Au sang versé de la révolution
La fuite périlleuse de Marc Brunel

Un exilé en sûreté, un lointain pays
Ouvrant de nouveaux chemins
Imaginant la marque de Brunel

Des forces qu'il ne pouvait chasser
La capitale lui a fait signe
Sa voix réclamant haut et fort Marc Brunel.

## Dig First, Think Later!

When money men came knocking there
Trevithick's head was turned
To dig for them beneath the Thames
Good living could be earned

Just mining in a different guise
Was all it seemed to be
Once hunting awkward Cornish coal
He'd dug beneath the sea

Armed with shovel, rusty pick
And recklessness wholehearted
Determined he to execute
The madcap scheme he'd started

Sardine tight yet sure of mind
Big heart Illogan giant
Digging out from Rotherhithe
Upon his God reliant

But came a day well past halfway
With satisfactory progress
When one last swing his piercing pick
Brought catastrophic ingress

Turning tail they upped and fled
A thousand feet the distance
Trevithick bringing up the rear
At his selfless insistence

Such task was deemed impossible
And ne'er will it be done
Risk and effort all to waste
Dead end, what he'd begun.

## Seizing Life

In the troubled reign of third King George
This day is born a Portsmouth son
New seconds tick, then seem to wait...
With Solent air clean lungs inflate
To rise, to never be outdone
With fervent aim, great dreams to forge.

## Sharp Practice

And so to rural Battersea
Mind awash with latent thought
A sawmill next the water's edge
To mass produce his honest pledge
Came Marc Brunel new patents sought

From roughest trunk straightest plank
His fine veneers keenly bought
As sturdy straight boots eased their pain
Trench foot soldiers fought again
Engaged, the Waterloo onslaught

By debt and hellish fire devoured
So furious no man to quench
Reluctant government paymaster
Ugly double edged disaster
Imprisoned he, at dour King's Bench.

## Way Beneath

Home a musty prison cell
Taxes due, his debt unpaid
The nation's waste of Marc Brunel

Time that concentrates the mind
Forming fast a mental plan
Slow incarceration grind

To dig and burrow as the mole
The wide the tireless Thames
Men inside a rabbit hole

Dig the silt pass the spoil
Water cascade run like hell
Fanciful dreamer Marc Brunel.

## Unrealised

From London through to Portsmouth
  a splendid waterway
The guarded thought of Marc Brunel
  one fertile thinking day
Yet frequency of gradient
  would thwart his unique flare
To engineer so many locks
  a cost too great to bear

A fittingly grand suspension bridge
  for Royal Kingston Town
Yet who to finance such a scheme?
  who'd lay their money down?
A multitude of brilliance
  would never see fruition
Such genius before its time
  could often court frustration.

## Ultimate Bore

Father Thames not the happiest fellow
Twist turning through London Town's heart
Having bridged me with brick stone and willow
It now seems that boring will start

Your lighter and oarsmen astride me
Their blasphemous tones I can take
But shovel and pick woe betide thee
One hell on Earth's mess will I make

Just who is this crass Brunel person?
Who schemes with his son Isambard
A tunnel, what possible reason?
May their going be devilish hard

Silt sand and filth upon them will rain
Till such day that they give up and go
Their hard won advance, their digging in vain
Leaving me to my unhindered flow.

**Short Cut**

Ring out, ring out, St. Mary's bells
Lies Wapping there, a thousand feet
At Rotherhithe the French Brunels
Sure as night two shores will meet

So near always yet still too far
By London Bridge five mile
The cursed thought and deed bizarre
Such angst to reconcile.

## Teredo Navalis

Encountering a soft shipworm
Teredo Navalis
The inspired mind of Marc Brunel
Dreamt metamorphosis

Inching inch by putrid inch
Inside the river's bed
Manmade Navalis eats its way
Through God knows what, instead.

## The Rainhill Rattler

Steam engines with firemen of note
their high speed prowess to promote
although slower of course
than a cantering horse
the same tender touch would devote

With grinding of chain around sprocket
one owner sped past in his Rocket
and by measured wit
mixed with northern grit
kept the trick up his sleeve, in his pocket

Soon to nobody's real surprise
there was prevalent boiler demise
the Rocket excluded
so the judges concluded
that on her they'd bestow the first prize.

## Health and Safety

At the Tunnel Company's behest
We hereby order, not request
Our lavish banquet you attend
The success of which will all depend
Upon the fickle Thames

We'll wait until the tide is out
To lessen pressure round about
With music by the Coldstream Guards
A splendid night is on the cards
Please wear your finest gems

The arches are an eerie sight
By flicker candelabra light
In the event of muddy feet
Just make your way up to the street
And wait for further news

But if things prove to be much worse
Should we fall foul the dreaded curse
Abandon quickly forks and knives
Then swim with vigour for your lives
And keep tight lipped your views!

## 'CANNON CAN BE NOTHING TO IT'

Suddenly up went a shout
roaring water and mud all about
as if through a funnel
a leak in the tunnel
was filling it quickly throughout

Isambard stood admiring the din
as the cold river came rushing in
although danger was rife
he escaped with his life
but the margin for error was thin.

## Trial and Tribulation

A brick tunnel under the Thames
is the sweetest of old London gems
and was dug straight through hell by the Family Brunel
who encountered unending problems

Having voiced his royal approval
Marc's head was due for removal
by taking such stance he was forced to flee France
on a knife edge his very survival

Trevithick advised Marc Brunel
there'll be woes too many to tell
you'll never reach Wapping without your heart stopping
so vile and putrid the smell

Soon after arriving from France
he decided on taking a chance
and promptly dug down beneath Rotherhithe Town
poor transport links to enhance

To his patented tunnelling shield
he felt certain all gremlins would yield
but conditions were dire as it cut through the mire
and a century's filth was revealed

Then old Marc Brunel nearly swore
as the water consumed his great bore
creating a beach all around Limehouse Reach
as the Thames was sucked into its jaw

Isambard whose instincts were mixed
by a thunderous roar was transfixed
with the dead more than five he was hauled out alive
quite living and dying betwixt

Their tunnel although problematic
at times was often dramatic
in declaring the roof to be quite waterproof
both father and son were emphatic

Now almost two centuries on
with horse driven cart long since gone
the railway train lights his tunnel again
most visible landmarks outshone.

## Canterbury and Whitstable
## (The Oyster Line 1830)

With joyous pride cathedral bells
   announce the railway
But few the miles to Whitstable
   this memorable May
Hang the bunting tree to tree
   strike up a happy band
Charge Invicta smoke and fire
   to sunny seaside sand

Young Stephenson the engine power
   old Stephenson the track
Complacent those who'll be devoured
   by hillside tunnel black
Mere few have travelled faster yet
   than sprightly horses run
What fate awaits their person here
   is shortly to be done.

## Young Lion

Laid low by tiresome injury
Thames Tunnel engineer
Impatience gripped the young Brunel
Sensing fame was near
As others seized initiative
Credentials to enhance
The fine mind like a coiled spring
Prepared to take its chance

'tween Liverpool and Manchester
Was greatest progress made
Where pioneering Stephensons
Put others in the shade
Yet soon the pent up Isambard
Desired to intervene
Unleashed, this wounded animal
Would burst upon the scene.

## Clifton Caper

Come span for us the limestone gorge
Cried Bristol's merchant men
Our balance sheets are in decline
Run dry red ink till then

Get for us the finest minds
Masters of grand design
Have them draw their daring plan
With castellation fine

Bring us Thomas Telford
And perhaps the young Brunel
We hear his tunnel escapade
Is faring none too well

From Stephenson we rarely hear
It seems he favours trains
Our bridge supports the horse and cart
Suspended there by chains

Impressive the suggestions
Of such eminent engineers
Brunel by some way boldest
Eliminating peers

But riots have the town consumed
And money men have fled
Alas our bridge a distant dream
Gives way to cold bloodshed

Flow east flow west great Severn Bore
Un-mounted yet our challenge
We will return with funding new
By hook, by crook, by scavenge.

## The Highwayman

'Now stand and deliver
   your money or your life'
Announced the dandy highwayman
   unto the old squire's wife
Springing large from hedgerow ditch
   in front of coach and four
To seize her flashing diamond ring
   and many treasures more

The road then but a dusty track
   from London west to Bath
Where ne'er do wells and bandits
   traversed its eerie path
To cutlass wielding highwaymen
   the scourge of olden day
An unsuspecting traveller
   would readily fall prey

Quite terrified those gentry folk
   the looter's whim obeyed
A day or two till journey's end
   by coaching inn delayed
Wayfarers roaming turnpike roads
   to hunt ill gotten gain
Toying with the upper crust
   themselves to entertain

At dusk a bulging mail coach
   raced over Shooters Hill
With musket primed and ready
   they homed in for the kill
Discarding packets on the top
   for better underneath
Coins of gold were shared amongst
   those brigands on Blackheath
When a knight in shining armour came
   in the form of the railway
Stealing stalking highwaymen
   had seen their last payday.

## 'LET ME TRY'

Having ridden 'board their railway
I arrived at this conclusion
Rattles shakes and lack of speed
Were suffered in profusion
Given time and half a chance
My thoughts will bring improvement
The logic of a wider track
Will make for better movement

How daring of the Stephensons
To opt for coal mine gauge
Their imagination backward
In a forward thinking age
Not far the time I do believe
When my scheme comes to flower
Where coffee will be surely supped
At forty miles per hour,

'LET ME TRY'...

## Avon Audacity

Victory in this great contest
By noblemen suggested
Will welcome recognition bring
And warrant time invested
To bridge somehow the yawning gorge
Audacious seems their plan
Although a fearsome task it looks
My instinct says I can

Without question it will be done
My spirit knows no bounds
I'll venture where no other dare
For fear there are no grounds
I visualise the finest lines
That merge with scenic beauty
To compliment, not to upstage
The engineer's first duty

In spite of Mr Telford's view
My thoughts will break new ground
No time or place for faint hearts here
His staid restraint renowned
I have upon my drawing board
A slender deck suspending
Eleven hundred feet in length
Is what I am intending.

## Telford Tenacity

The function of the railways
So Telford once explained
Will be to serve my waterways
His thinking pre-ordained
Harboured he strange Luddite thought
Self preservation firmly sought

Proposals for a Clifton span
Placed mighty Menai in the shade
With one at nearly twice the length
His noble prowess to degrade
So doyen Telford called a halt
A wave of jealous pride his fault?

His own design in haste submitted
All other entries cast aside
To Menai Bridge span length committed
The ugly plan, they would deride
Gone that spirit of adventure
Un-tarnished though, his golden tenure.

## Suspicious Survey

Dawn till dusk 'stride chestnut mount
In haste each country mile to count
Cloak and dagger Inn to Inn
True reason secretive within

O'er landed gentry holding sway
Their ample tracts to prise away
With promise of an ornate bridge
Of first class views across the ridge

Long searching for a level way
Their land a meagre price to pay
To barter hard with lord and duke
At all dissent to cock a snook

We have our 'one in thirteen twenty'
Our legal Bill our land aplenty
Sell up be gone without delay
The Company will have its way.

## Iron Dream (1833)

Get off your land cut down those trees
My trains are coming through
Scoff if you wish but by degrees
My men will see you do

Stop digging all those waterways
Pack up and work for me
I'm building broad gauge railways
Your narrow barge set free

Lay down that rein of leather
Embrace the age of steam
Gouge deep through gorse and heather
Then live my great iron dream

Divert your stream and footpath
Let sheep and cattle graze
Why laze around a warming hearth
Through pioneering days?

Build my stations high and grand
Extend their platforms long
Where passengers will proudly stand
In joyous gleeful throng

Via bridges and through tunnels
Over viaducts of style
My new Great Western Railway
Will shrink the English mile.

## Cock-a-Hoop

Fair brimming with patience and tact
Brunel gave them detail and fact
his manner quite bold
was a joy to behold
when debating the Railway Act

And many the folk gathered round
were in raptures when Parliament frowned
from the young engineer
neither panic nor fear
for running, had he hit the ground.

# Cut and Thrust

*(some of the many possible obstacles to be overcome at both planning and building stages, by those attempting the construction of a permanent way in the early to mid-nineteenth century, in either fair weather or foul)*


Poor ground at Hanwell sinks and shifts
Near chaos has ensued
And Mr Hoffenden's garden wall
Too far it does protrude
The 'Feathers' stands on Ealing Green
Its land adjacent seized
Our new track bed must run straight through
'tween pub and turnpike squeezed

The route's secure from end to end
All land purchase agreed
Though some monies have been withheld
Quite wrongfully indeed
Our Engineer his heels drag
Himself no businessman
Just authorises payment when
Faced with an access ban

When Isambard with eagle eye
Found bad bricks on the meadow
He looked to find the culprit quick
God help Grissell and Peto
Yet soon a stunning viaduct
From grazing land should rise
Nine hundred splendid feet in length
High into Middlesex skies.

## Cruel Progress

By manmade inland waterway
Tow and prosper laden barge
Through iron trough aqueduct convey
Wrath inducing steep toll charge
Tired feet that knew dark tunnel wall
Soon trudged new railway track install

Completion of the final arch
A celebratory cigar
Mead flagon quenching summer's parch
Lofty Wharncliffe landscape scar
Tortuous their back break pang
Toil and graft Great Western gang

Infamous Brunel broad gauge
Bold testament to much intent
Thrusting spirit of the age
Across the cowslip meadows of Brent
With scant regard for how things were
Slow silt and die Grand Union spur.

## Sign of the Times

The Wiltshire white horse was their pride
cut clean on a chalky hillside
as they valued the trade
from a coaching route made
the Great Western they couldn't abide

Replace the white horse with a train
someone challenged Brunel with disdain
being a good natured man
he drew up a plan
all malice from which to refrain

Take with you string, shovel and spade
he ordered his ten man brigade
under cover of night
cut a train in full flight
concealing the horse with turf made

But for all his charisma and flair
it seems he thought it unfair
so they never awoke
to that practical joke
perhaps even he didn't dare!

## Industrial Revelation (Stations West)

Grand days when only time advanced
Canal and horse power slow suffice
Passing decades few enhanced
Tall wind blown sail imprecise
Same perspective year to year
Satisfactory simple pleasure
There came to pass an engineer
Whose radical thought defied measure

Tedious Parliamentary act
Railway shadow looming large
Fenced land snatched in one way pact
Journey's end, clean equine barge
Little thought to delegation
Smallest detail overseen
Isambard self-regulation
Cautionary signals always green

From flooded bores at Rotherhithe
To flattest arch for Maidenhead
Westward ho embattled scythe
The Brunel footprint fearless tread
Dizzy new industrial height
Majestic Wharncliffe viaduct
New cutting edge burning bright
Impervious cast iron aqueduct

Gunpowder hollowed Box Hill rock
Few tears shed for good lives lost
By candle light around the clock
Hard heads dismissing human cost
Perpetual shift work regimentation
Doss house bedding never cold
Horrific ear drum perforation
Hideous stories rarely told

Rail gauge width bitter wrangle
Engine speed trials won with ease
Wretched bureaucratic tangle
Many scorned his latest wheeze
Broad gauge stole execution stay
Much standard track already down
But narrow minds would win the day
Cheap jewel raid on the Brunel crown

Timber spans for quick assemble
Funding scarce near Tavistock
Temple Meads gothic resemble
Element sheltered rolling stock
Brisk Swindon heavy engineering
Boundless pioneering zest
Tamar cleared, completion nearing
Greenwich Meantime all points west

Official opening, modest fanfare
Subdued Victorian excitement
Great Western Rail breadline snare
Cheapest third class fare enticement
Early setbacks quickly righted
One man's dream another's hell
A visionary so far sighted
Isambard Kingdom Brunel.

## Cat of Nine Lives

Spectators became horror struck
Isambard in a basket was stuck
in the iron rod a kink
with his life on the brink
he summoned unwavering pluck

From Leigh Woods and Clifton dismay
they gasped at his fearless display
then chattered with glee
as the tangle came free
'twas typical Brunel horseplay.

## Doctor Dogma

Although Dionysius Lardner
Felt utterly certain he knew
By woefully poor calculation
Made five from two plus two
Lesser individuals
Heard and believed all he said
But the day he challenged I.K.B.
He should have remained in bed

A ship of iron might try to sink
He warned the great engineer
Yet Archimedes Principle
Would duly interfere
The passengers aboard your train
Will suffocate at speed
If brakes should fail on a slope
They'll perish, yes indeed

The genius mind of I.K.B.
Had long suffered many a fool
Though never gladly, he'd admit
And reluctantly as a rule
But bumbling Dionysius
Had broken untrod ground
Weak theory came to haunt him
As to his cost he found.

## Shipping Lines

Grand liners steaming through the past
Successors to the age of sail
Paddle then screw replacing mast
Great hull of iron tamed fiercest gale

Fine wooden ship fully evolved
Ultimate beauty Cutty Sark
Old industry with change involved
Technique emerged from ages dark

Knowledge gained from bridge construction
Yet still untapped the Brunel mind
Formidable his rare deduction
Much old convention left behind

Aloud read he the shipwright's play
Re-writing script on every page
Tyne, Clyde and Mersey joined the fray
But Isambard stole centre stage

New energy and enterprise
Hurry scurry stovepipe hat
Ships of stature, ships of size
Long revered his shrewd format.

## Smoke for Sail

The Queen announced a Bill this day
Regarding Royal Mail
Across oceans and far away
Must word and packet sail

A problem does exist of course
Such schemes tend to defy
We have no ship just humble horse
Beg Mam please clarify

To India one hundred days
America somewhat less
How long on lazy listless seas
I'll hazard not a guess

Her Majesty though young of crown
The coming world has seen
Where glowing coals force sail down
Long live our noble Queen.

## Significant Shift in Somerset

One hundred feet its generous span
   a shallow twelve the crown
The bridge they built on Parrett mud
   was slowly falling down
Two years the arch supported
   by ample timber frame
But Brunel said dismantle
   before collapse day came.

## Sandcastle Science

Doctor Lardner the prophet of doom
delivered a lecture with gloom
there were coughs and sniggers
as his 'facts' and figures
were announced to the listening room

He proceeded to pontificate
upon matters of power and weight
because the U.S. of A.
is so far away
much coal will oust people and freight

Yet even with greatest fortune
her fuel will expire way too soon
and the Great Western ship
into dire straits will slip
'One might as well try for the moon'

Remaining polite in his seat
later Isambard took to his feet
as usual his claim
was ahead of the game
and the good Doc was forced to retreat.

# Head Start

At four days out, the Sirius
Fought big Atlantic swell
On fire steam ship Great Western
Below, a smoking hell
Slipping through a hot charred rung
Crashed Isambard Brunel
Twenty feet into her bowels
Straight onto someone fell

A spent force soon, the Sirius
Chairs to her furnace thrown
White sail fluttered aimless
And slowly westward blown
Quickly bringing up the rear
With deficit unknown
Great Western relished heaving seas
Much coal her cornerstone

Full steam her threshing paddle
Sprayed daring lines of oak
Endowed with fuel aplenty
And coppered hull bespoke
Limping home tired Sirius
Most fittings up in smoke
Blue riband though Great Western
To you, New York awoke.

## Maidenhead

Two arches wide of hard fired brick
You span the timeless Thames
Elliptical illusion trick
A kingdom's brightest gems

Majestic trundle broad gauge steam
Ixion firebox check
Now stately standard diesel gleam
Comes thundering your deck

Brunel tones, a voice steadfast
Through whistle winds of March
Call from distant decades past
To haunt your sounding arch.

## 1 in 233

In Avon Gorge by Clifton
  a predicament exists
The 'helpful' views of others
  his intention to resist
Construct the bridge deck level
  and it will appear to fall
A yard the drop toward Leigh Woods
  his foresight to install

The illusion of angle
  creates a complication
Making necessary
  this unusual intervention
They flocked to toast the genius
  of Isambard Brunel
Who stormed the heights while others
  soon by the wayside fell.

# First Great Western

We men have set his track in place
Our fingers to the bone are worn
He's torment writ across his face
Upon our work he pours his scorn
At five foot six in stovepipe hat
He has the navvies quaking
Floors us with that vicious chat
His every moment waking

From Hanwell up to Maidenhead
We graft at early dawn
Seven days a week he said
You'll hardly know you're born
Embankment finished payment please
No use gentle persuasion
He's brought our guv'nor to his knees
On more than one occasion

Fair galloped on his charcoal steed
To meet a Mr Newman?
Near eighteen hours to Temple Meads
We sometimes doubt he's human
To ride aboard his train our plan
Reward for sweat and toil
But Brunel says we never can
'cos we're neither rich nor royal.

## Pushing Boundaries

Steam ship Great Western full ahead
   by fractious waters tossed
Rein in and take yon Sirius
   defeat her at all cost
Challenge of the smoking stacks
   rise up and grasp the nettle
Go ply with ease those fearsome seas
   Atlantic duel to settle
Hidden safe from sight
   across a grey horizon line
How great the closing deficit
   not easy to define

With near disaster conquered
   and three days in arrears
Captain Claxton at the helm
   a true trajectory steers
For fourteen anxious days and nights
   of Sirius no sign
Gone forever any chance
   that lead to undermine
And so for her New York at last
   just slender hours to spare
Thus concludes this version
   of the tortoise and the hare.

## It's Not Quite as Broad as it is Narrow

Much anger and confusion
  in the battle of the gauges
The Royal Commission's findings
  could run to several pages
Such incompatibility
  is bordering on farce
Reasoning void of common sense
  the idea logic sparse
Mr Brunel's argument
  is keen and forward thinking
That faster trains need broader track
  is based on more than inkling
The length of narrow gauge track laid
  is six times that of broad
And any implication drawn
  just cannot be ignored
Brunel's gauge has proved itself
  to be the best throughout
Yet this will soon be sacrificed
  of that seems little doubt.

## Legendary Letters

Long letters written at furious pace
Angry overtone quite commonplace
Of cynical wit, much more than a trace
Precise, concise all in good grace
No flatter or frill,
From Isambard's quill...

You must move this station a foot to the right
That girder of iron sits at the wrong height
No place here such inaccurate blight
You'll right every wrong no matter how slight
In for the kill,
Stormed Isambard's quill...

In a brief fit of lapsed concentration
I arrived at the wrong calculation
You will study this new illustration
Then act on its clear information
With cast iron will,
Wrote Isambard's quill...

It is vital we seize every chance
My great standing in life to enhance
Take the toughest possible stance
And inform me of any advance
With keenest skill,
Scribbled Isambard's quill.

## When Great Minds Differ

What good can ever come of it?
In thoughtful moment wonder
Railways of differing gauge
Has logic come asunder?

Through cutting deep, embankment high
Brunel runs seven feet
While further north they've four foot eight
What happens when they meet?

Why such pointless quest for speed?
Who minds how long things take?
They always get there in the end
Why care for goodness sake?

This railway thing is with us now
Strange how the world seems faster
Still waterway has had its day
White steam cloud's lord and master

So out to grass keen young Shire horse
Let go flat bottom barge
Make way for Mr Stephenson
May the mighty Rocket charge

Just don't forget to tell Brunel
His broad idea's all wrong
It's Stephenson who'll win the day
He could see it all along.

## Moles

Yellow white each flash of light
Sudden day lights deepest night

Pressured waves of sulphurous air
Snuffing wax pool candles there

A dull reverberating hum
Repeats through perforated drum

Blinding splintered stone cascade
One grudging inch of progress made

Bloody searing red raw lung
Too soon old the eager young

Claustrophobic tomb of rocks
Expendable, the moles of Box.

## Silly Money

That bungling magician Brunel
had the young children under his spell
when the coin on his tongue
dropped into his lung
he felt just the slightest unwell

He coughed loudly at twenty past four
then at seven he spluttered some more
with his small frame inverted
a sharp shake exerted
the lost gold rolled onto the floor.

## The Box Brigade

One thousand strong, they marched on Box
With hope enough to break the rocks
In charged they with powder stocks
Behind the General

Two thousand strong, with iron will
Long yards inside that grass green hill
Their fortitude unbroken still
Bravo the General

Three thousand strong, their lungs aflame
Cut down in hoards and him to blame
An enemy too wild to tame
Despite the General

Four thousand strong, they knew the light
That reached to them from left and right
Bright day retrieved from blackest night
Hail the General.

## Stress Strain and Temper

The quality of iron cast
   is clearly below par
My presence at the foundry
   improves standards by far
In general this material
   does not command my trust
Its reckless use in bridge span work
   fills me with disgust

The patternmaker's skilful craft
   deserves much recognition
His accurate and clever mould
   a masterly creation
Dusty blueprints on the bench
   breed sand impression shapes
From honesty and excellence
   he seeks not to escape

The foundry man however
   is a weak link in the chain
With hole and imperfection found
   time and time again
Wrought iron with its tempered strength
   is coming to the fore
This engineer's confidence
   to enhance and restore.

## Paddington Bare

Through Severn mist shone Temple Meads
Unmatched the London end
Drab wooden shed at Paddington
Could not the Board defend
Plain cake without an icing
That went against the trend
A situation stemming from
Great Western overspend

Smart stone for rural Chippenham
At Pangbourne much the same
With Swindon, Bath and Steventon
All worth their high acclaim
Yet when compared, the Capital
Appeared distinctly tame
Slim chance their spendthrift Engineer
Would shoulder any blame.

## We of Little Faith

Our Engineer has built for us
A bridge so reckless in design
We hardly risk to even sneeze
Lest brick and track to Thames consign
All centering to stay untouched
In place it must remain
Such thought to him seems ludicrous
It goes against the grain

Some miles further down the line
A bridge from timber cobbled
On angled fans of raking beams
The worm should feast untroubled
His stations built to grand design
Have eaten all our money
The folly gracing Temple Meads
Is neither fit nor funny

We'll send the line to Cornwall
Should our shareholders vote yes
Just how he'll cross the Tamar mouth
Is anybody's guess
Many of his grand ideas
Are way too far progressive
Some future century perhaps
Today they seem excessive

His science tends to baffle us
We know not what he speaks
The railway must open soon
Not in months but weeks
Common sense and broad gauge track
Were kept at his insistence
With resignation on the cards
Had we displayed resistance

A bridge above the turnpike road
Soon cracked neath stress and strain
Its cast iron structure failed him
We did not dare complain
In its place a timber deck
With one small oversight
Hot coals from a passing train
Soon set the wood alight

He smokes those dreadful fat cigars
His health is on the wane
As much as forty every day
Perhaps we seem mundane
He hardly ever goes to sleep
We cannot understand
How any other human being
His workload could withstand

In spite of many differences
It seems he'll pull us through
His like may not be seen again
In old worlds or in new
We hereby wish to make them known
Our thoughts of one accord
And thank him for a sterling job
By order of the Board.

## Paternal Perception

Isambard dear Isambard
  you'll work yourself to death
Each day through and often night
  till your last living breath
Head aloft in hopeless times
  great dreams to contemplate
Belief in grandiose idea
  no thought to deviate
They seemed impossibilities
  your 'Castles in the air'
Of style and beauty boundless
  vision beyond compare
Don't let them undermine your will
  or wear you down my son
Of battles fought, few battles lost
  most often battles won
That youthful face is showing age
  too soon before its time
Learn trust and delegation
  reclaiming then your prime.

## 'IF I EVER GO MAD'

The railway has caused much strain
    but soon will be complete
'Blue devils' lured him to the brink
    he now sees their retreat
To countenance one wasteful day
    was never once considered
Every waking hour filled
    with thought and deed untethered
The tunnel proved so troublesome
    one hundred men are lost
Brave lives given for the cause
    don't justify such cost
Decisions so momentous
    are not easy to defend
His little devils haunting him
    right to the bitter end.

## Amused

Her Majesty, enamoured with
The new Great Western line
Wonders if a branch could serve
Her stately castle fine
Upon the billiard table track
She travelled filled with zeal
Rides to which she duly gave
A reigning monarch's seal
To Windsor over royal bridge
Would be her greatest joy
So if the Board could stretch a point
She'd smile, then long enjoy.

## 'UPWARDS OF 100 MEN'

At the post event enquiry
Into injury and death
They muttered of the working man
Beneath their high class breath
The blasting of Box Hill near Bath
Gave ragged hordes employ
For that they should be grateful
Be they man or be they boy

Conditions in that place of work
Were roughly those expected
The means to safeguard life and limb
As yet to be perfected
All injury regrettable
No record where or when
The number killed uncertain
'Upwards of 100 men'.

## Time Motion Tabled

For the purpose of the railway
We wish to make it known
That different time along its route
Will all become one zone
Discrepancy from east to west
Is causing complication
We therefore deem this plan the best
From long deliberation

For you the wealthy traveller
There will appear no change
Do not adjust your timepiece
Or think the idea strange
Reading Berks. to Temple Meads
Equates to seven minutes
The constant turn of planet Earth
Governing all within it

The benefit of Railway Time
Will soon become apparent
All station clocks as one will chime
Our master plan transparent
Sit back relax but do not sleep
Absorb a visual drama
The vivid memory yours to keep
Of English panorama.

## Graphic Guide

When travelling the railways
In town or countryside
Near or far 'tis always wise
To go with Bradshaw's guide

From:
Huntingdon to Harpenden
Rickmansworth to Rhyl
Temple Meades to Tenterden
Or Hayes to Haverhill

Ilfracombe to Ivybridge
Shoeburyness to Sheen
Berkhamsted to Boroughbridge
Then Grays to Gretna Green

Ambleside to Amersham
Craven Arms to Crewe
Brightlingsea to Birmingham
And Hyde to Herstmonceux

There are long trains short trains
Full trains and empty trains
To smokey towns pokey towns
And jokey towns beside
So only dare to venture there
When armed with Bradshaw's guide.

## Modification Ramification

After somewhat short contemplation
And possibly flawed calculation
Isambard's engine configuration
Was received with due consternation

The locos, a motley collection
Ran poorly without an exception
Daniel Gooch with advice and suggestion
Brought vision and valued perception

Coaxing boilers of no inclination
With seemingly small alteration
His work meeting little objection
Continued producing perfection

To detail closest attention
All strictly in line with convention
Though timely his wise intervention
The cure cost more than prevention.

## In the Vale of the White Horse

So once a week to Steventon
Trooped members of the Board
In railway business to engage
With thought of one accord

The furtherance of prospects
To seek a higher rung
At this the mid-point east to west
Spoke they with silver tongue

Distant meetings far from town
Away from prying eye
Many a log to warming fire
Cigar and spirit high

Short lived those times at Steventon
Much jovial time afforded
Though all such 'special business' went
In minutes, unrecorded!

## Glorious Great Britain

Down at Great Western Dock there are changes to changes
He's abandoned the paddles along with the oak
Is there no end to Isambard's forceful endeavour?
Or the slightest regard to cost whatsoever
Reckless his actions, red ink to provoke

Just to see and to marvel, they come in their numbers
Wrought iron and rivet, the Shipwright's new art
Layman's eyes witnessing modification
Bristolians ponder the ramification
Only lock gate dismantle ensures her depart

Mr Brunel the Victorian Noah
Sheep, cattle, ships cat, pink pig and fowl
His seaborne menagerie rides trough and crest
Commanding the high seas north south east and west
Around six sturdy masts strong Southerlies howl.

## The Engineer

The engineer of mighty mind
Parameter and limit blind
Accepted thinking redefined
All barriers torn down

Visionary sixth sense plan
Casual walk where peers ran
Momentous quest consumed the man
Linking town with town

Gravitational law deceived
Impossible spans conceived
A God-like wisdom they perceived
Clear writing on the wall

'Upwards of 100 lives'
Alms subsist, Great Western wives
Brass fanfare his soul revives
North Star broad gauge haul.

## Nautical Nadir

It is indeed a travesty
   their treatment of my ship
That somehow from her plotted course
   they let Great Britain slip
Those fools mistook a beacon light
   then quickly lost their way
Hence amidst the black of night
   so far her wake did stray
That now their view of Ireland
   is from sandy Dundrum Bay

Left to battle wind and wave
   her hapless form deserted
To face the fret and fury
   by winter storm exerted
The building of a barricade
   might give her half a chance
By lessening the impact
   of a charging sea's advance
It is in fact our only hope
   to take this desperate stance.

## Under Pressure

The highs and lows of gradient
Will instantly strike fear
Into the very soul
Of any railway engineer
One foot in seven hundred
And he hardly seems to care
Yet one in ninety seven
Has him tearing out his hair

So our man came down Devon way
To check the rise and fall
And soon devised a cunning plan
That baffled one and all
A train without an engine
Will go at greater speed
That extra locomotive weight
Just what it doesn't need

An iron tube of generous width
Was laid between the line
And early indications showed
That everything was fine
With pumping stations sited
Both up and down the track
The vacuum power created
Pulled coaches there and back

His brittle leather seal though
To rats was falling prey
Upon its tallowed surfaces
They had a field-day
With pressure in the pipe too low
Shareholder pressure rose
He looked to cut his losses quick
Or so the story goes.

## Refreshment?

The coffee at Swindon met scorn
it left him feeling forlorn
an Isambard letter
said he'd tasted much better
and to him it resembled roast corn

So in future when taking the train
from that beverage bound to abstain
he has serious doubts
about those lacklustre grouts
swearing never to touch 'em again!

## The Ghost of Dundrum Bay

An unexpected visitor
Once came to Dundrum Bay
Looming out of misty seas
Unplanned, her lengthy stay

High and dry on golden strand
Great Britain came to rest
Run aground by lunatics
Constructed by the best

Aghast her puzzled audience
In disbelief stared they
Their beach a rusting scrap yard
On bended knee to pray

The Good Lord quickly intervened
With best help soon at hand
Brunel in dandy stovepipe hat
Came storming down the sand

Heads hung low in hopelessness
Much theory was expounded
What to do, where to start?
In silt a fathom grounded

Although departed many moons
The locals to this day
Will sometimes see neath heavens bright
The ghost of Dundrum Bay.

## Credible Concept
## (Devil's Bridge, Uphill)

Mr Brunel's flying bridge
   of character and grace
Leaps a leafy cutting
   in some pleasant summer place
Arching high the rail bed
   so sleek and daring slender
Springing keen from angled slopes
   in broad elliptic splendour
Guaranteed abutment free
   an art form quite simplistic
Devil's Bridge at Uphill
   hangs imposing and majestic.

# Gremlins at Newton Abbot

In Devon they soon reached a stage
where terrain was unfit for broad gauge
but he'd learned of a way on a Dublin foray
of enhancing the railway age

'twas the wrong kind of slope for a train
no engine the power to sustain
so with options few he puffed and he blew
yet who was Brunel to complain?

Though rarely defeated before
he met peeving frustrations galore
fine pump houses there fought hard to draw air
from a pipe of quite ample bore

Many problems and snags to address
on Isambard's vacuum express
when in summer weather some rats ate the leather
it was deemed not his greatest success

So the scheme to a farce was reduced
nothing like enough power produced
coerced and caressed it still failed the test
and must cease forthwith he deduced.

## Isambard's Important Industrious Innovative Ivybridge Improvisation Idea Inevitably Implemented Immediately

Our viaduct at Ivybridge
It scares folk half to death
Having mustered great courage
Close eyes then hold their breath

Carried pier by slender pier
This high above the ground
The railway we hold so dear
Feels neither safe nor sound

Some don't dare to risk the chance
They wouldn't ride for free
Others take a different stance
They trust in I.K.B.

To doubt is hardly feasible
The time has come I'll wage
Where anything is possible
In this enlightened age.

## Railway Racket

A railway mapped by 'The Hat'
was near billiard table flat
one in thirteen twenty
its scant rise aplenty
six sixty the fall after that

Yet the men laying Great Western track
were quite often under attack
even rare praises sung
by that sharp acid tongue
were akin to a knife in the back

While deep in a tunnel of rocks
they were cursing the blasting shocks
though he just couldn't say
when the bright light of day
would shine on those brave moles at Box

Their footplate and firebox aglow
his troublesome engines seemed slow
with scarcely the force
of a runaway horse
quite why he just didn't know

What old Stephenson couldn't abide
was rail gauge seven feet wide
the price you will pay
is that I'll win the day
poor Isambard he would chide

Then in voice of single accord
uttered the Great Western Board
we're delighted the track
goes to Bristol and back
not a single yard of it flawed!

## Suspension of Belief

To market, to market, to Hungerford market
To market place over a death riddled Thames
Vile the waste on an ebbing tide shore
A million the black rats of needle tooth jaw

To market, to market, through miasma summer
Where great gleaming chains leap a cauldron of filth
Searing the hot pang of cholera death
Its stranglehold tightens round every drawn breath

To market, to market, forever to market
Someday somehow bad waters will clear
With lost fish and heron returning there
Brunellian faith signals hope in the air.

## The Chepstow Challenge

Brunel's bridge plan for Chepstow
   far exceeded known design
In order to clear fifty feet
   above the waterline
The engineer fair racked his mind
   an answer to produce
By severing restraints
   let his imagination loose
Of girder, plate and iron truss
   the unique form consisted
Proportions so unusual
   no name for it existed

A century of heavy use
   fulfilled the common good
Quite why it had to be replaced
   not fully understood
'twas only he who could have dared
   to jump that awkward gap
Thus placing ancient Chepstow
   more firmly on the map.

## Travel Fever (1850)

The Railway boom is at a stall
   shares are on the wane
And never will such frenzied feed
   repeat itself again
The country's linked from end to end
   side is joined with side
Ridden upon by one and all
   with eagerness and pride

Permanent Way is uniform
   the gauge war has been won
His seven foot experiment
   not mourned by anyone
In less than half a century
   we've reached this heady stage
A nation living in the past
   brought to the modern age.

## Leviathan

My plan to build a mighty ship
Is treated with derision
To launch her broadside on the Thames
It seems creates division
Much old thought unchallenged goes
Too free the blind acceptance
I pause to question everything
This often breeds resistance
The shadow my good ship will cast
Could shade an East End street
Their hearts will leap in wonderment
Her presence indiscreet
My judgement says the shipping world
Is anchored in the past
A world of oak and sail where
Such scornful glance is cast
But what know I of Starboard talk?
Displacement or propulsion
The workings of the seven seas
They fear I'll bring convulsion

To sweep away a thousand years
Of wood built non-advance
Will lift them from their dull malaise
I ask of them the chance
A mere builder of bridges I
Landlubber to the last
Theirs the tested expertise
Honed skills with knowledge vast

But I will take their world apart
Then skew their comprehension
Two plus two will soon make five
I'll alter their convention
My ship made of toughest iron
Traversing soon the globe
Her paddle, screw and wind filled sail
Will every corner probe
Now point me at the shipyard
And let begin the fun
Then watch the old world marvel at
What I, Brunel have done.

## A Meeting of the Board at the Eastern Steam Navigation Company

Gentlemen,

There is but a single item
   on today's agenda
Any vote in favour of,
   is certain to be slender
For discussion is a ship
   of quite immense proportion
Causing most Board members
   fear of financial distortion
In Mr Brunel's wild plan
   he asks us to believe
Not something we mere mortals
   can readily perceive

Amongst our number gathered here
   an air of apprehension
Giving rise to muttering
   and angry interjection
A ship six times the current size
   of anything afloat
Upon such aberration
   we now prepare to vote
To follow heart? To follow head?
   scant guidance from within
Does Brunel slip a straining leash
   or do we rein him in?

## The Crystal Palace

With ware and product to display
Beneath glazed acres in the Park
Great Exhibition of the day
Excessive Victorian lark

Came plan and daring new design
From worthy engineers of note
High reputations on the line
Along with silken shirt and coat

From pompous stovepipe hat brigade
Spoke Paxton, Stephenson and Fox
Career enhancement their crusade
Trumped by Brunel on tall soapbox

His the splendid water towers
That sprang from grassy Sydenham slope
Devouring countless waking hours
In endless thought of broadest scope

But fiercely glowed that London night
To molten pools ran Screaming Alice
His mighty towers remained upright
A sullen end for Crystal Palace.

## A Shipwright's Challenge
## (The Testing of John Scott Russell)

My dealings here through recent weeks
Were tiresome to say the least
I've been persuaded to construct
Some vast great monstrous metal beast
A Mr Brunel strode in here
With thought and fancy plan
A ship of iron if you please
He is not an easy man

I am master of this trade
Revered and much respected
My ships have voyaged all seven seas
Not one of them neglected
The finest vessels leave this yard
A joy for captain as for crew
Pure product of our expertise
I WILL NOT BE SPOKEN DOWN TO

So let him have his modern ship
Let queen and country gather
Ten deep from here to Greenwich Park
With little for their bother
A single thing is guaranteed
Once Millwall mud has settled
She'll bring financial ruin to
Those folk long years embattled.

## In Order to Aid the Good Works of 'The Lady With the Lamp'

Deaths of wounded troops abroad is cause for deep concern
This high rate of mortality the problem to discern
To ship a temporary hospital would suit the situation
Creating thus the new concept of mass pre-fabrication.

## One London Winter

When black the shades of autumn amber
Came flurries then of early snow
Trudged far the hardened ragged masses
Through sharp tooth gale heads dipped low
From dank rat holes in Mile End
From Silvertown and Bow
Surged they the mighty ship to fashion

Came hungry kids from roughneck alley
In bone chill fog white rivets danced
No Christmas cheer for thieving urchins
'mongst ringing caverns young lives chanced
By stealth through searing months of winter
In size the greatest ship advanced
Broad tidal slope its form devoured.

## Undignified Demise

Her masts cut down and under tow
   Great Western faced the end
That one time eager greyhound
   cleared Blackwall's sweeping bend
In sombre slow procession
   past a mournful Isambard
Presiding o'er Great Eastern
   at the edge of Russell's yard

Of swift Atlantic crossing
   once the undisputed queen
A trail blazed for others
   to follow where she'd been
Away with stout sea worthiness,
   with craftsmanship sublime
The grates of London drawing rooms
   glowed bright that winter time.

## Industrial Revelation (King of Iron)

Through shady East End soot and grime
Rare optimism on the vine
A chance to break from petty crime
Dogs' shipyard winning contract fine

Down muddy flats near Limehouse Reach
Paced the fiery stern Brunel
On mission new to pry and preach
Great iron ship stories quick to tell

The certain clash of mighty minds
Inevitable mental tussle
Frustrated Isambard soon finds
Ice rarely cut with Shipwright Russell

Then devastating fire consumption
Models templates drawings lost
Smouldering ember, slow resumption
His shipyard groaned neath rebuild cost

From ashen waste great Phoenix rising
Constant drawing board returns
Terraced hovel rooftop towering
Through winter's fog pale lamplight burns

Handcart wheel on smooth worn cobble
Wrought iron plate dragged by the score
White hot rivets at the double
Shirkers gruffly shown the door

Wily kids between the plating
Narrow gaps where men don't fit
Leviathan monster them creating
Cunning duck dive streetwise wit

Project finance called to question
Banks and lenders closing in
When Brunel offers no suggestion
Stark silence ousts metallic din

Receiver skilfully placated
Great Eastern nears the finish line
Tickets sold, grand launch awaited
Ensuing farce, theatrics shine

Hopeful champagne, ironwork foaming
Grudging yield half a yard
Distractive throng Brunel bemoaning
Neither hand held one ace card

Attempts to clear the Thames mud trap
Too numerous and dull to mention
To break her up and sell for scrap
Was it seemed, their new intention

Then brightest moon on highest tide
Floating free her silted shackle
With luck not judgement on their side
Relief replaced raised angry hackle

Midst splendid opulence unrivalled
Their very lives five stokers gave
By searing steam blast them bedevilled
Her haunted maker sought his grave

Long years before his true intention
Passenger take-up woeful sparse
Sea cabling her new vocation
Before ship breakers cease the farce.

# Cathedral

Fine glasswork at Paddington station
an inspired Brunel sensation
its imposing presence
Crystal Palace in essence
pure offspring of Paxton's creation

Gleaming sunlight shafts through the roof
play brightly on harness and hoof
by cast iron at its boundary
from a Midland foundry
ride Butler with Lady aloof

No wish to endure the brass band's
cacophonous sound from the stand
so onward in haste
not a moment to waste
somewhat harsh its particular brand

Stowing luggage and valuable case
then into a plush first class space
in this new golden age
on his splendid broad gauge
whisked away to some West Country place.

## Controlled Launch Paradox

We grease the ways, we slacken chain
Then barely half a yard she'll slip
Yet cursed mud and driving rain
They dampen not, his showmanship
To Shipwright Russell... most unwise

Come every dawn this ritual
Yearning we, that lifting tide
But all seem ineffectual
Not one thing left to man untried
To Shipwright Russell… no surprise

The 'free' launch option his preferred
And many times he firmly stated
Yet Brunel won when they conferred
Imagining such thought outdated
To Shipwright Russell… disbelief

She floats, she floats, their joyous cry
Three cheers for Isambard Brunel
No longer stranded high and dry
What stories grandchildren to tell
To all concerned… a great relief.

## Ship of Dreams

I've a maritime story to tell
of Isambard Kingdom Brunel
his men hammered rivets while he took the plaudits
in working conditions from hell

Brunel demonstrating defiance
could baffle his critics with science
your ship will not float his detractors would gloat
demanding his every compliance

From a shipyard at Millwall on Thames
came the finest of Isambard's gems
the Great Eastern ship would its rivals outstrip
yet cause him unending problems

The launch proved a terrible strain
years of struggle and effort in vain
poor Brunel was aghast when in mud she stuck fast
a large crowd to long entertain

Until by some pure lucky chance
on the highest of tides did advance
beneath a full moon she was gone none too soon
his position in life to enhance

The great ship around Margate slew
when one of her vast boilers blew
the unfortunate five were soon boiled alive
though little about it they knew

Yet when she was holed neath the water
not a single lamb to the slaughter
and things were not frantic out in the Atlantic
as with Titanic fifty years after

But the Company books were a mess
she was not a commercial success
years ahead of her time, never reaching her prime
they dismantled his ocean empress.

## Turner Technique

From artist's sable trap released
Squat smudge locomotive blur
Leaping large from lavish light
With not a care for Mr Hare
Sprinting both, the reckless span
Obliquely double crossings fan
Yet truly parallel indeed

RAIN STEAM AND SPEED.

## The Effort of Equals

A nervous Robert Stephenson
In need of some support
Called upon his steadfast friend
With tension growing fraught

Britannia's great iron tubes
Above Menai must rise
Now visions of the Dee collapse
Appeared before his eyes

Compelled to help his 'equal'
Brunel lent expertise
Fair bristling with confidence
His presence bringing ease

Shoulder leaned on shoulder
Perfection ousting flaw
The rivalry of equals
Each others strengths to draw.

## Georgian Wind Victorian Reign

Fat cigar neath high top hat
Tall orders barked sunrise till set
Rivets girders and digging that
Ensured their shirts were dripping wet
Chain link backdrop photo shoot
Society contacts swiftly gained
Though wary of their new recruit
Great East West visions soon explained

Persistent bouts of brilliant thought
Deciding what the nation needed
Vivid dreams then finance sought
All pessimistic views unheeded
Bridges tunnels broad gauge rail
New iron shipping out at sea
From travellers to Royal Mail
All lives touched by I. K. B.

Flat metal rail threaded west
No fool stood or quarter given
Broad gauge track, no second best
Slavishly each worker driven
Sulphurous poison within Box Hill
Deep Tamar water's dreaded Bends
With dozens dead and hundreds ill
The Penzance prize all anguish mends

Blueprints lost as shipyard glowed
Project jinxed right from inception
Opinions differed progress slowed
Human loss met poor reception
Exploding rams shattered chain
Blackwall silt Great Eastern inching
Red flag white flag little gain
Havana puffer never flinching

Launch attempt, vast crowd encroachment
Fine wine breaking way too soon
Peacock strut, top hat adjustment
Passed several phases of the moon
Stokers caught steam pressure blast
White elephant on sunset sea
Cable layer to the last
The top hat rests... I. K. B.

## Watershed

To rise in time from red Devon earth
Aside sapling of cedar of beech and of ash
Whimsical Watcombe spectacular birth
Pure fantasy of utmost panache

Grand chateau conceived of fertile thought
When alarmingly life's summer decays
From burdensome load quiet solace sought
A place to reflect through halcyon days

Worsening health in terminal plummet
Steep terraced landscape eager to root
Callously cut down close to the summit
Utopian pipedream never to fruit.

## Hamoaze Hurdle

How to cross the wide Hamoaze?
The burning question of the day
A timber span the great man said
As options few engulfed the head
His drawing board in disarray

But swiftly swirled those waters deep
How daunting seemed a fast run tide
That lesser mortals would defeat
New headroom of one hundred feet
The Admiralty specified

And so to rock midway across
His mighty caisson sunk with verve
Though ravaged by the evil Bends
His iron will their plight transcends
Through thick and thin he held his nerve

Great tubular prefabrications
Raised aloft the waterline
A rivet there of purest gold
Old Saltash legend little told
'I. K. BRUNEL. ENGINEER. 1859'.

## Confounded Conclusion

I realise now my time is short
Yet unfulfilled remains ambition
I see at last what others saw
Knowing now what they have known
To death I've worked this flesh and bone
Exhausted to the very core
Surrendering without condition
How simply galling seems the thought.

## A Directive From the Office of
## I. K. Brunel Esq. Duke Street London

Mr Brunel has gone away
  his ailment to ease
He suffers from a rare condition
  known as Bright's disease
He succumbed to doctor's orders
  such was the demand
So please direct your business
  to his second in command
His understudy Brereton
  a wise and thoughtful man
Is blest with deepest knowledge
  and will help you where he can.

## Sabbatical

This vital trip abroad to bask
   in warmer foreign climes
To counter and perhaps reverse
   the strain of former times
A body that is faltering
   tortures an active mind
And restless days breed endless nights
   as Isambard would find

He'd been 'laid up and useless'
   way back in early days
Due to injury sustained
   from young impulsive ways
But this time it was illness
   that had struck and laid him low
Something which control over,
   he'd not the slightest though
Meanwhile back in England
   things continued to progress
Some day soon the opening
   of major bridge success
He'd miss the pomp and pageantry
   Prince Consort for the Queen
The splendid Saltash structure
   'mongst the finest ever seen

His pride and joy Great Eastern
  from maiden voyage just weeks
On his behalf down by the Thames
  an understudy speaks
Is the pressure he'd applied
  being constantly sustained?
The rallying of weary troops
  are standards being maintained?
These were the very pressures
  that had led to his decline
Long years of tireless battling
  his health to undermine
Despite the beauties of the Nile
  intrigue of fine landscape
From these his worldly duties
  there could be no full escape.

## Sundown

Lenticular black silhouette
Across the Saltash sunset lies
Resultant of its maker's hands
Old masterpiece in autumn stands
Sublime against red western skies.

## INEVITABILITY

INCURABLE ILLNESS, FAILING HEALTH
WARM CONTINENTAL CONVALESCE

ORGAN ROBBING HIM BY STEALTH
CIGAR SMOKE TOLL, WORKLOAD STRESS

WITH SALTASH MASTERPIECE COMPLETING
ITS SIGHT PERHAPS HIS SWEETEST DAY

SOMBRE BEDSIDE FAMILY MEETING
IN TRANQUIL CALM…

HE SLIPPED AWAY

# End to End

From Britain Street to Harrow Road,

A pathway of objective
A pathway of experiment
A pathway of incentive
A pathway of accomplishment
A pathway of perspective

From Britain Street to Harrow Road,

A journey of intention
A journey of wonderment
A journey of invention
A journey of astonishment
A journey of distinction

From Britain Street to Harrow Road,

A lifetime of ambition
A lifetime of possibility
A lifetime of intuition
A lifetime of capability
A lifetime of fruition

From Harrow Road to...

## Passing Era

It is indeed the cruellest blow
To family and profession both
That in the shortest span of time
Two engineers of eminence
Messrs. Brunel and Stephenson
Their assertive gaze no longer cast
O'er landscape of potential vast
An industrial phenomenon
Ideals steeped in excellence
Steam harnessed, ironwork sublime
Enabling transportation growth
First pointers of the way to go.

## Earthly Estate

Although a healthy sum was left
   vast wealth did not abound
A fortune made a fortune lost
   in ventures less than sound
The mighty ship a money drain
   down which Brunel poured cash
And other risky strategies
   reduced the family stash

Investment wisely chosen though
   had more than saved the day
His shareholding in railways
   a guaranteed mainstay
The ninety thousand pound estate
   put there for her to find
Meant luxury and comfort
   for the wife he'd left behind.

## Boycott

At the opening of Clifton Bridge
   no Brunel will assemble
Aspects of the finished span
   do not his plan resemble
We see here little evidence
   of Father's grand design
And therefore do not wish
   his memory to undermine.

## American Aberration

Sea empress gashed off Sandy Hook
How all but she would surely die
As paltry tin her iron plate
Steadfast a posture to belie
Listing wounded ocean queen
Her darkest caverns filling high
Feverish, New York awaits

Distraction lured and overtook
The process of a tiring mind
Leaving to the hand of fate
That far, that faint metallic grind
With not a fathom in between
Yet endless water out behind
A future jinxed, she contemplates.

## Lively Legacy

Eleven days America
   they cheered the power of steam
Near seven hundred bow to stern
   and eighty 'cross the beam
Great Eastern toyed with serpent seas
   defeating wind and wave
While quite impeccable throughout
   her every effort gave

The haunt of rich and famous
   preserve of precious few
Passengers a rarity
   far outnumbered by crew
Most crossings running at a loss
   the company in debt
Brunel long since departed
   though not easy to forget

Communications suddenly
   the order of the day
For Sheerness Kent they made in haste
   without undue delay
When stowed there in her ample hold
   a mighty cable drum
The inter-continental
   message service had begun.

## Dickensian Pied Piper

Disease and death in London Town
Two centuries beyond the plague
With many thousand going down
Causes argued solutions vague

Sewage outflow street and alley
Filthy fester poisoned Thames
Insufferable needless folly
Fish and otter long lost gems

Stealthy black rat dockside scurry
Hourglass grain sack running free
Wapping, Limehouse, deadly slurry
Frenzied feeding rodent glee

Up dead end streets to market driven
Scrawny livestock bloody slaughter
Red run cobble entrails riven
Deformed cretin's crazy laughter

Weils tainted Empire roots
Atlas pink lands ruled by rats
Cholera foothold, tough green shoots
God implored from stained prayer mats

Plucked from post in marshland reclaim
For urgent work in dying town
Came Joseph Bazalgette of strange name
Hawking plans for deep deep down

When Parliament folk could take no more
Rarest Common's sense prevailed
Dickensian banish to the fore
Brick lined sewer soon unveiled

Lethargic limbs rejuvenated
Yesterday, the foul air frown
Populace invigorated
Declared Pied Piper of renown

Rodent headcount shrink and dwindle
Health and well being steepest rise
Water board ceased wicked swindle
Clean supply both poor and wise

Bazalgette served London's needs
His subterranean labyrinth
For this, and many other deeds
'Sir' Joseph and Embankment plinth.

## Falkland Faux Pas

When deadly skies turned fearsome dark
Shuddered she, the ageing ship
A furious tempest charged her down
Fierce latitudes around the Horn
Where snarling waters angry raged
Mere twig, windjammer mast akin
For never in such guise perceived
Left for dead on Southern seas

Faux pas on Southern seas.

## Narrow Minds

Short years since the Gooch resistance
Championed the Brunel cause
Three rails kept at his insistence

Railway landmark etched the mind
From Paddington slipped the Cornishman
Broad gauge track ripped up behind

To go, though never to return
From grace the falling final
Rain grew weed where hot coals burned.

## Exhibitionism

In their wisdom, English powers
Ruled Crystal Palace water towers
Could there no longer stay

Lest early in the second war
Their presence then and evermore
Should give the game away

Yet in the Park to thwart their cause
Enormous concrete dinosaurs
Remain until this day!

## Doctor Beeching Goes off the Rails


The man from the ministry came just to see
He appeared almost human actually
Stood on the platform counting to ten
Then just to be certain he counted again
He winced and he frowned at the 8.42
To Southcroft via Westchurch with passengers few
Red hot glowing firebox, the hissing of steam
Her green and gold livery, sparkle and gleam

Good morning he muttered Beeching's the name
And I'm here to observe this futile game
In dismay he moaned at the state of the track
The strength of the tea and the taste of the snack
Old grey station master he stooped to attention
Then bowed and saluted too often to mention
Not even the polished and oiled sack barrow
Cut any ice with the mind of the narrow

The trees were too short, the flowerbed too tall
The ashtray too square and the tickets too small
I'll report what I've found at the next A.G.M.
His important strut seemed God-like to them
A whistle blew somewhere from over the hill
Then a billowing white cloud engulfed the old mill
There were sighs of relief as he boarded the train
Thank you your worship please don't call again!

## Simple Sentiment

At Paddington bad news to tell
to a silent non-ferrous Brunel
he was taken aback
by the width of his track
its narrow gauge not boding well

But I'd plenty of keen information
of tunnel of bridge and of station
and he seemed quite glad
I hasten to add
at the praise of today's generation.

# Regardless

Too many the sleepers that rot in the brambles
Too weak the voices that uttered dissent
Too savage the actions of impulsive thinkers
Too short the time till they'd crack and repent

Too few the people in far away places
Too unimportant their everyday needs
Too headstrong those with power unbridled
Too rash by far were their dastardly deeds

Too dark the light at the end of the tunnel
Too deaf the ear when they sought to complain
Too loud to ignore though, the voice at St Pancras
Too keenly contested, the poet's campaign

Too busy and bleak is the motorway concrete
Too full the lorry, too empty the car
Too dirty their lungs in the town and the city...

Too long ago, was the railway star.

## Monumental

Ghosts of timber viaducts
 haunt still, the stark terrain
Thin mossy piers of granite stone
 pierce Cornish skies in vain
Monuments to far off days
 stand proud and yet forlorn
Aside their modern counterparts
 of all importance shorn
Of angled fans, sufficient deck
 no solitary sign
Inexpensive excellence
 met gradual decline.

**Second Great Western**

Walking Paddington station the feeling was pride
Having paid him due homage along platform side
As I paused to imagine what dead decades hoard
Brunel's bronze expression said welcome aboard
Rich purples and pinks line the glass covered acre
Bog standard the track so despised by its maker
I saluted you Sir as I glimpsed Kensal Green
Still your presence abundant, if so long unseen
Through Ealing to Hanwell and places beyond
Atop Maidenhead arches of trustworthy bond
Passing Betjeman's Slough and moving apace
His harsh but true words adding shame to disgrace
Long gone an excuse for inaccuracy
Once Reading's four minutes became G.M.T.
Dear o dear Didcot great towers of concrete
Neath their shadow unnoticed, forever a backseat
Industrial Swindon less busy these days
Its waterline deep holed by Thatcher malaise
Soon through his great portal deep into the rocks
Where one hundred ghosts roam the tunnel of Box
Awaiting its turn and next in our path
Lies the dignified splendour of Georgian Bath
Then back where they sowed those original seeds
Not two hours elapsed…

    spick and span Temple Meads.

# Sweet September (2010)

The car it seems, has had its day
In Central London anyway
So pedalled I in autumn sun
'cross Wandsworth Common leafy still
September gust blows strong until
Those final bronze leaves cascade down

When walkers block my cycle lane
Their dogs at least show better brain
Till over busy Bolingbroke
Through switchback streets of yellow stock
Late Clematis and Hollyhock
Elspeth and Latchmere I then took

But Albert Bridge not quite so grand
Through plywood walkway work in hand
Scaffold, cable, blue hard hat
Will 'CYCLISTS PLEASE DISMOUNT"
Though bus and car on no account
Its old age rusting to combat.

Defunct power stations left and right
Near sweeping bend their former might
'Moving' landmarks trick the eye
As angles change neath shifting sky
On Cheyne Walk my hunt begins
With blue plaque research for my sins

Two centuries since they were here
The French Brunels lived somewhere near
Smart terraced line in Georgian days
From end to end walking the bike
My search reveals nothing like
No symbol here to sing their praise

So in the early afternoon
I leave this place of silver spoon
Of CCTV trained doorway
Across a bridge by Bazalgette
This timeless river's fine asset
A fruitless yes, but pleasant day.

Great Western Railway – cutting at Sydney Gardens

Great Western Railway – The Royal Hotel at Slough Station

# EXPLANATORY NOTES

**Emigré (page 8)**: French royalist Marc Brunel was forced to flee his country in 1793 to escape the Revolutionary forces. Boarding a ship bound for America, he stayed there for nearly six years before coming to England to be reunited with the girl he had left behind when abruptly leaving France. Mr Brunel and Sophia Kingdom were married on 1st November 1799 at Holborn, London.

Fleeing the Rouen fires of hell
From spilling blood and revolution
The perilous flight of Marc Brunel

Exiled safe, a distant land
The carving out of pathways new
Envisaging the Brunel brand

Powers he could not dispel
The greatest city beckoned
Its voice called loud to Marc Brunel.

**Dig First, Think Later (page 9)**: Cornish mining engineer Richard Trevithick attempted but failed to complete the digging of a tunnel under the River Thames at London in 1807, some years before the Brunels began, then eventually completed, their Thames Tunnel which today carries the London Underground between Wapping and Rotherhithe.

**Seizing Life (page 11)**: Isambard Kingdom Brunel was born on 9th April 1806 at Britain Street, Portsmouth.

**Sharp Practice (page 12)**: Soon after the birth of third child Isambard, Marc Brunel moved his family to Lindsey Row, Chelsea, London on the banks of the River Thames beside Battersea Bridge. His sawmill business was set up directly opposite the house on the south side of the river. The premises burned to the ground in 1818.

**Way Beneath (page 13)**: Although Marc Brunel was an inventive genius, his attention to matters of business was sadly lacking. When the Government failed to pay promptly for army boot orders correctly dispatched, or even at all, the operation ran into trouble. Mr Brunel soon fell into debt and found himself unfairly imprisoned. It was during this period of incarceration that ideas of a tunnel under the Thames began to form in his mind.

**Teredo Navalis (page 17)**: When Marc Brunel studied the large soft shipworm *Teredo Navalis* boring its way into ships' timbers at Chatham Dockyard, the first seeds of a tunnelling shield were sown in his brilliant mind. Once completed, an improved version was used to bore the Thames Tunnel.

**The Rainhill Rattler (page 18)**: The Rainhill Trials were held at Liverpool in 1829 to determine the best way to progress with the newly invented railway steam engines.

**Health and Safety (page 19)**: In order to demonstrate the safety of their unfinished tunnel to the public, the Thames Tunnel Company, at the suggestion of Isambard, held a lavish banquet inside it one night in November 1827.

**'Cannon Can be Nothing to it' (page 20)**: 11th January 1828 saw the worst of many breaches of the Thames Tunnel. Isambard, present at the time, was spellbound by the roaring sound of the incoming water. The title of this poem is his own words. Six men were killed in the incident; although badly injured he only narrowly avoided being the seventh.

**Canterbury and Whitstable (The Oyster Line 1830) (Page 23)**: The city of Canterbury saw great celebrations on the sunny morning of 3rd May 1830. A new railway linking it with coastal Whitstable six miles to the north was about to be opened by the mayor in all his finery; it seemed the whole city had turned out to witness the occasion. The line engineered by the now legendary George Stephenson at a cost of £31,000 was preceded only by the Stockton & Darlington and the Liverpool & Manchester railways (both his), far away across horse drawn England.

Although relatively short at six miles this line was a feat of engineering in its time, containing a half mile stretch of 1 in 31 gradient and a tunnel over one thousand yards long through Tyler Hill near the Canterbury end. Passengers in open wagons were pulled by Robert Stephenson's *Invicta* engine, built in 1825, which resembled his father's *Rocket*, complete with the tall thin chimney of its predecessor, between the line's only two stations on this inaugural trip.

By the late 1830s, having worked the track for nine years, Stephenson's little *Invicta* was ready for retirement and sold off. An experimental atmospheric traction system was tested on the stiff climb towards Tyler Hill tunnel although not adopted. The railway quickly became known as 'the oyster line' after Whitstable's famous product and remained in existence until closure circa 1953. Although there is little to link this fairy tale railway to the Brunels, legend has it that Isambard, then a young man in his twenties, once paid a visit purely for observation purposes.

**Clifton Caper (page 25)**: Bristol Alderman William Vick died in 1753 leaving £1,000 in a bequest to the Society of Merchant Venturers, stating that once this initial sum had grown with interest to £10,000 it should be used to fund the building of a bridge across the Avon. In 1829 with the fund standing at £8,000 it was found that nearer to £90,000 would be needed, and a competition was launched to attract designs for a bridge that could be built for a more reasonable sum.

**Avon Audacity (page 30)**: Following recovery from injuries inflicted in the Thames Tunnel accident, Isambard experienced a lull in demand for his professional expertise. It is thought he travelled to Bristol after hearing of a competition inviting designs for a bridge to cross the River Avon at Clifton.

**Telford Tenacity (page 31)**: Having already built the splendid Menai suspension bridge which opened in 1826, Thomas Telford was deemed the man to judge entries for the Clifton bridge competition.

**Suspicious Survey (page 32)**: Isambard Kingdom Brunel beat rivals to become Engineer to the Great Western Railway in 1833. He travelled on horseback between London and Bristol to map out the route and secure the necessary land along the way, remaining secret at all times about his business there, thus keeping the cost of land purchase to a minimum. 1 in 1,320 refers to the average gradient of the section between London and Swindon.

**Cut and Thrust (page 35)**: The construction of the first major landmark on the GWR out of Paddington, the magnificent Brent, later to become Wharncliffe, Viaduct at Hanwell. Due to a minor oversight at planning stage, work was temporarily halted when the garden wall of a Mr Hoffenden in Church Lane was found to be in the way of proceedings. Messrs. Grissell and Peto was the chosen contractor to construct the eight arch viaduct. Today, in addition to its GWR duties this structure also houses a colony of rare bats.

**Cruel Progress (page 36)**: The age of the canal as the main means of distributing goods across the country was drawing to a close and the manpower involved in the building of these waterways was preparing to switch its skill to the construction of a successor – the railway.

**Sign of the Times (page 37)**: The good folk of a Wiltshire village (probably Cherhill), were said to be proud of the white horse cut into a nearby chalk hillside that overlooked them. They made a living from coach traffic on the Bath Road and as a result were angrily opposed to the coming of the Great Western Railway. Someone suggested to Isambard that it might be amusing to replace the horse with a steaming white locomotive sporting giant letters GWR underneath.

Liking what was said, he immediately set about producing one of his renowned sketches, then appointed a ten man team to carry out the jape the following night. However, it seems Isambard had second thoughts and the prank didn't materialise. By pure coincidence Wiltshire is the county that has suffered most from the crop circle craze of recent times.

**Cat of Nine Lives (page 41)**: In August 1836 a wrought iron rod 1,000 feet in length was placed over the Avon gorge at Clifton, in order to transport building materials from one side to the other. To draw attention to the worth of this idea the ever flamboyant Isambard climbed into a suspended basket to be pulled across by rope. A kink developed in the rod at the halfway point and he became trapped there for a time, more to the horror of the watching crowd than to himself.

**Doctor Dogma (page 42)**: Doctor Dionysius Lardner was the self-professed expert of the day on many matters scientific and would belittle new ideas on a regular basis; especially those of I. K. Brunel whose thinking was often so far ahead of its time that to some, may have seemed almost ridiculous.

**Smoke for Sail (page 44)**: A light-hearted reference to The Postage Act passed in 1839.

**Significant Shift in Somerset (page 45)**: The attempted brick bridge over the River Parrett in Somerset was one of only two failures for Isambard, the other being a cast iron skewed bridge spanning the Uxbridge Road near to the site of the Wharncliffe Viaduct at Hanwell. Neither incident claimed life.

The abutments of the Somerset Bridge gradually spread apart in soft ground and the order was given for it be taken down two years after completion. Brunel designed in excess of 1,000 bridges, the exact figure is unknown.

**Sandcastle Science (page 46)**: Although Dionysius Lardner was a leading scientist in his time he was prone to mistake. The thinking of the day regarding steam ships was that power input would need to increase in line with size. For example, if a ship of 1,000 tons displacement required a 200 horse power engine, a ship of 2,000 tons would need 1,600 horse power to achieve the same performance. Isambard, realising this to be wrong, bravely challenged accepted theory.

Lardner, however, was slower to recognise the fact, claiming that due to an inability to carry enough coal it was not possible for a steam ship to reach America from Bristol or Liverpool, adding famously that they might as well make a voyage from either port to the moon. Unfortunately for him, it is for this metaphorical statement that the Doctor is best remembered.

**Head Start (page 47):** The *Great Western* steamship was delayed by a fire aboard while still on the Thames at Canvey Island, before attempting to become the first ship to cross the Atlantic powered by steam in 1838. Mr Brunel was badly injured and failed to make the crossing. Although rival *Sirius* reached New York first, almost everything aboard that was combustible had to be thrown on to the furnace, such was the lack of coal reserve. *Great Western* completed the voyage in 15 days, three less than her rival.

**Maidenhead (page 48):** Perhaps Brunel's most daring structure, the Maidenhead Viaduct carrying the GWR over the Thames in Berkshire consists of two main semi-elliptical arches spanning the actual river, which is approaching 300 feet across at this point. Each arch is 128 feet wide, the crowns of which rise to only 24 feet above the waterline, and are thought to be the flattest arches in the world to this day.

**1 in 233 (page 49):** Because of the differing angles at which the land descends into the Avon Gorge from both sides – almost sheer from Clifton, nearer to 45 degrees from Leigh Woods – Mr Brunel deemed it necessary to introduce a slope of three feet into the deck of the Clifton Suspension Bridge rising towards Clifton at an angle of 1 in 233. This, he said, would make the deck appear level when viewed from a side elevation. One is not aware of this rise/fall when walking the bridge.

**Pushing Boundaries (page 51):** The race in 1838 to be first across the Atlantic in a vessel powered by steam. It is worth noting that *Sirius*, due to her relatively small size (700 tons), and therefore inability to carry enough coal, relied heavily on sail power to see her through.

**Moles (page 55)**: The blasting of the nearly two mile long Box Tunnel between Chippenham and Bath took five years, claiming the lives of many. At an inquiry after completion, the question was asked about the number killed during construction. Proper records, however, were either not kept or destroyed. The short and vague answer given was, 'Upwards of 100 men'.

**Silly Money (page 56)**: The accidental half Sovereign swallowing episode occurred at a children's birthday party where the versatile Isambard turned entertainer.

**The Box Brigade (page 57)**: During the course of digging the Box Tunnel, its work-force was gradually increased in number in order to speed up completion which took five years from 1836. The early months of 1841 saw a monumental effort to finish the job. 4,000 men were employed using one ton each of gunpowder and candles per week with up to 300 horses taking away the spoil.

**Stress, Strain and Temper (page 58)**: Mr Brunel was no fan of cast iron when used in the long lengths required for bridge building, and would sometimes cite Robert Stephenson's Dee Bridge failure as an example of the material's unreliability.

**'If I Ever Go Mad' (page 64)**: In letters to trusted friends, Isambard occasionally referred to his 'Blue devils' or feeling 'Blue devilish'. Presumably sometimes feeling tortured in a similar way to Winston Churchill who spoke of a 'Black dog'.

**Amused (page 65)**: It is thought the GWR Company was approached on behalf of Queen Victoria, to have a short branch constructed from the main line at Slough, serving Windsor Castle; such was the monarch's enjoyment of the new railway.

**Time Motion Tabled (page 67)**: The introduction of 'Railway Time' in 1840 was designed to simplify timetables, or indeed make them even possible.

**Modification Ramification (page 69)**: Steam engine expert Daniel Gooch was brought in by GWR to determine why engines designed by I K Brunel were underperforming. He quickly decided to increase the diameter of the blast pipe which carried exhaust gases away from the engine, thus releasing their full potential.

**In the Vale of the White Horse (page 70)**: A fun look at the weekly Board meetings of the GWR held at Steventon station (closed in 1962), which was nearest the middle point of the line, thus keeping travelling time to a minimum for Directors from either end. This early arrangement was to last a mere six months or so!

**Glorious Great Britain (page 71)**: The SS *Great Britain* was initially to be a wooden ship of 2,000 tons, powered, like her predecessor SS *Great Western,* by paddle wheels. At a stroke Brunel changed the specification – she would be his first iron ship. With work well under way on the hull he is said to have witnessed another smaller vessel pass by that appeared to have no obvious means of propulsion. An investigation revealed the source of power to be a screw propeller.

A halt was immediately called to all work on Brunel's ship, and the hull modified to incorporate this latest form of propulsion. Meanwhile the use of iron increased her weight to 3,443 tons. Brunel's propeller proved so efficient in design, that those powering today's ships are better by no more than five per cent.

Voyages to distant lands took so long in early Victorian days, that the SS *Great Britain* carried with her the only means available at the time of feeding passengers and crew with fresh produce – live animals!

**Under Pressure (page 74)**: One of Isambard's few unsuccessful ventures. The Atmospheric system on the South Devon Railway, designed to cope with steep gradients, was abandoned after only one year. The idea, although not his, failed because a suitable material did not exist to form a good seal in the vacuum tube.

**The Ghost of Dundrum Bay (page 77)**: Due to navigational error, Brunel's ship SS *Great Britain* ran aground on Ireland's east coast in 1846.

**Credible Concept (Devil's Bridge, Uphill) (page 78)**: The 'Flying' bridge utilises the angled faces of a cutting instead of abutments to contain its single arch against collapse. The crown of the 115 foot wide arch at Uphill, North Somerset is some 60 feet above track level. These slender bridges were built near to ground level, and once completed, the full extent of the cutting was then excavated to the required depth. Another example of a flying bridge can be found at Liskeard station in Cornwall.

**Gremlins at Newton Abbot (page 79)**: Another reference to the Atmospheric system on the South Devon Railway.

**Isambard's Important Industrious Innovative Ivybridge Improvisation Idea Inevitably Implemented Immediately (page 80)**: Mr Brunel built numerous timber viaducts across Cornish valleys to carry his railway at a lower cost to the cash strapped companies that ran them. The viaduct at Ivybridge, although high at around 100 feet, came nowhere near the highest – that accolade belonged to the St. Pinnock at 152 feet. Although many of these timber spans lasted several decades, none survive today. However evidence of them still exists in the shape of slender masonry piers that once carried the timber framework and deck.

**Suspension of Belief (page 83)**: Isambard's Hungerford Suspension Bridge spanned the Thames from Lambeth on the south bank to Hungerford Market which stood on the site of today's Charing Cross railway station. This handsome footbridge was dismantled in 1860 to make way for the railway, which to this day is carried on a bridge that uses his original red brick and sandstone oval shaped bases. The chains were salvaged and used in the construction of the Clifton Suspension Bridge.

**The Chepstow Challenge (page 84)**: A short reference to the unique bridge at Chepstow built 1850-52 for just £77,000, which carried trains over the River Wye on the South Wales Railway. Although the actual bridge structure was to last 110 years, its replacement was built onto Brunel's original foundation work.

**Leviathan (page 86)**: The possible thoughts of Mr Brunel prior to the building of the SS *Great Eastern*.

**The Crystal Palace (page 89)**: The Great Exhibition of 1851 in Hyde Park, and eventual transfer to Sydenham, South East London. Brunel's elegant water towers (one at either end of the 1,800 feet long glass structure), were in excess of 250 feet in height.

**A Shipwright's Challenge. (The Testing of John Scott Russell) (page 90)**: The potential ponderings of one of the world's leading Shipwrights, who was awarded the contract to build the SS *Great Eastern* on The Isle of Dogs, London.

**In Order to Aid the Good Works of the Lady With the Lamp (page 91)**: After tireless campaigning by Florence Nightingale on behalf of wounded soldiers in the Crimea, the British Government consulted Mr Brunel who designed a temporary pre-fabricated hospital which was shipped out to Renkioi in Turkey eventually housing 1,000 soldiers. Its existence there from 1855 helped to drastically reduce the mortality rate.

**One London Winter (page 92)**: The building of the SS *Great Eastern* on The Isle of Dogs in the 1850s. Legend has it that when the ship was dismantled in 1888-90, the skeleton of a child was found between the double hulls.

**Undignified Demise (page 93)**: Whether or not Brunel was present on the Isle of Dogs the day SS *Great Western* passed by, heading upstream to the yard of Henry Castle at Vauxhall to be broken up is not important. The thought of him turning from his work to face the river at that moment is somewhat enchanting. There certainly is evidence that he took time off to visit his first ship during its dismantling. Steamship *Great Western* served an eighteen year working life.

**Cathedral (page 97)**: Mr Brunel undoubtedly drew inspiration from the glass building which housed The Great Exhibition of 1851, to design the roof of the new Paddington Station soon afterwards.

**Controlled Launch Paradox (page 98)**: John Scott Russell had strongly advised that the SS *Great Eastern* be launched in the conventional manner onto the Thames. The ship was longer than half the width of the river and Brunel, fearing she might collide with the opposite bank, insisted on a broadside or controlled launch. This difference of opinion caused great conflict between the two men.

**Turner Technique (page 101)**: A personal though unpopular opinion! *Rain, Steam and Speed*, Turner's famous painting of a GWR locomotive crossing the Maidenhead Railway Bridge.

**The Effort of Equals (page 102)**: The raising of the first great iron tube of Robert Stephenson's Britannia Railway Bridge across The Menai Straits in 1849. Brunel is said to have considered Stephenson a rare equal to himself, and although professional rivals were always good friends to each other.

**Watershed (page 105)**: Brunel purchased his first tract of land at Watcombe near Torquay, Devon in 1847 with a view to building a fine French Chateau style house in which to eventually retire with his family.

**Hamoaze Hurdle (page 106)**: Hamoaze; the mouth of the River Tamar separating Devon from Cornwall. The bridge at Saltash was originally to be built from timber, carrying two broad gauge tracks. In the event it was constructed of masonry and iron, but narrowed to house only a single track in order to reduce cost.

**Inevitability (page 112)**: The death of Isambard Kingdom Brunel on 15th September 1859 at Duke Street, London.

**End to End (page 113)**: I K Brunel was born at Britain Street, Portsmouth on 9th April 1806. He was buried in the grave of his parents at Kensal Green Cemetery, Harrow Road, London on 20th September 1859.

**Passing Era (page 114)**: Renowned engineer Robert Stephenson died one month after Brunel in the autumn of 1859. The deaths coming so close together were a devastating loss to the engineering world.

**Boycott (page 116)**: As a memorial to Isambard, the decision was taken amongst surviving professional colleagues to complete the aborted Clifton Suspension Bridge. However, it seems even they did not quite trust the slender lines of his design, so the plans were not adhered to by them and many features were strengthened, resulting in the somewhat 'bulkier' yet still splendid bridge we admire today. This action caused anger amongst the surviving Brunel family.

**American Aberration (page 117)**: The holing of the SS *Great Eastern* off New York in 1862. Because Brunel had designed his ship with a double hull, a 90 foot gash below the waterline made little visible impact on her. She completed the voyage safely into New York with only a slight list, leaving most passengers completely unaware of the incident.

**Lively Legacy (page 118)**: The SS *Great Eastern* was never a commercial success as a passenger ship; the cost of a voyage was beyond all but the wealthy. However she came into her own in 1865 as a communication cable laying vessel, firstly laying the Atlantic cable. No other ship of the day was big enough to undertake such work; the drum measuring a massive 75 feet in diameter.

**Dickensian Pied Piper (page 119)**: Joseph Bazalgette was recommended to the Metropolitan Board of Works by one Isambard Kingdom Brunel.

**Falkland Faux Pas (page 121)**: After a lengthy working life as a passenger ship, the SS *Great Britain* was converted into a cargo vessel in 1882. Her engines were removed and she effectively became what was then termed a Windjammer. After taking a severe battering in a storm off South America in 1886 she limped into Port Stanley and was abandoned. Later the Falkland Island Company used the ship for storage, before it was scuttled decades later in shallow water after becoming too dangerous.

By 1970 enough funds had been raised to have her rusted hulk towed back home to her birthplace in Bristol, where, over a period of many years she was restored to her former glory. The ship is now on display to an admiring public.

**Narrow Minds (page 122)**: The dismantling of the broad gauge in 1892. Daniel Gooch became Chairman of GWR in 1865, and was a staunch supporter of Brunel's unique format which by then was running in conjunction with narrow or standard gauge by means of a third rail. It was therefore not until after his death in 1889 that the demise of this system could be contemplated.

**Exhibitionism (page 123)**: Although in sound condition, Brunel's water towers at Crystal Palace were demolished in 1940. The thinking being, that their presence could act as a guide to enemy bombers attacking London in the Second World War.

**Doctor Beeching Goes off the Rails (page 124)**: Whatever would Isambard have had to say? His reaction can easily be imagined: he gave his best years to building railways, only for a mere Doctor of Physics to bowl up and sweep many away at a stroke 125 years later. Had they both lived in the same age, Beeching would almost certainly have been sent packing. We can never know!

**Sweet September (2010) (page 129)**: A Blue Plaque containing the names of both Sir Marc and Isambard Kingdom Brunel is hidden from view behind a high brick wall on Cheyne Walk, Chelsea, London. The address of the home of the Brunels in the early part of the 19th century was known as 4 Lindsey Row, today it is 98 Cheyne Walk.

# ACKNOWLEDGEMENTS

My sincere thanks for assistance in the compilation of this book go to the following:

The GWR Steam Library for the supply of the six John Cooke Bourne lithographs used to enhance the book.

The Curator of the Library and Archive, SS *Great Britain* Trust, for access to the diaries and other related material of Isambard Kingdom Brunel.

The Clifton Suspension Bridge Visitor Centre, for historical facts concerning final completion of the structure.

To all who have endured my relentless enthusiasm for the subject matter over a long period and in particular those who have offered kind encouragement, especially Rosabel Fremantle and Christopher Simmonds.

To my son David for co-writing the poem, Isambard's Important Industrious Innovative Ivybridge Improvisation Idea Inevitably Implemented Immediately.

To my brother Andrew, for invaluable assistance.

To Sandrine Boehm, for translating the poem Emigré into French.